COVENTRY
CATHEDRAL

FRONT COVER: *Christ Crucified. This fine sculpture by Helen Jennings of Oklahoma, U.S.A., was fashioned from the metal of a crashed motor car. It serves to remind one that the daily crucifixions of man by man in careless driving, like those in war, can only be redeemed by love.*

ABOVE: *The old and the new. The shell of the ruined 14th-century church is linked dramatically to the new cathedral by the great canopied porch.*

FATHER FORGIVE

COVENTRY CATHEDRAL

H. C. N. WILLIAMS Provost of Coventry Cathedral

SACRED indeed is the ground upon which Coventry Cathedral is built. Hard by the west wall of the new cathedral are visible the bases of some of the massive buttresses which supported the great medieval cathedral. Joined to the new cathedral by the great porch is the 14th-century parish church of St. Michael, which in 1918 became the second cathedral. Hence the third cathedral stands as a massive link between the first and the second—a symbol of the indestructibility of the faith which it expresses.

Medieval Coventry was small, enclosed by a wall. Within this wall were many churches. The greatest was the Church of St. Mary's Benedictine Monastery, built in 1043. This church, when enlarged in the 13th century, was similar to and in fact larger than the present Lichfield Cathedral. Lady Godiva, wife of Leofric, Earl of Mercia, supported its foundation with considerable wealth. Further ruins of its walls are visible in Priory Row, to the west of the new cathedral.

Holy Trinity and St. Michael's churches were built in the 14th century. Their proximity to one another and to the priory itself is witness both to the prodigality of church-building at that time, and to the extent to which status was defended by those who claimed it. Holy Trinity was apparently built for the tenants of the prior's half of the town, and St. Michael's for the tenants of the earl's half of the town. An accident of history has, appropriately, named the roadway separating these two ancient churches "Cuckoo Lane". Now, however, Holy Trinity is the great parish church in the centre of the city, and its work and the cathedral's are entirely and happily complementary.

The third of the famous "Three Spires" is the ancient Christ Church near Greyfriars Green, but only the spire now remains.

As is evident from the building which must have taken place in the 14th and 15th centuries, of which these churches were brilliant and beautiful examples, Coventry was prosperous. It was indeed the principal market town of the Midlands, and it soon developed crafts for which it became world-famous—ribbon-making, leather and glass work, watch-making, and latterly every conceivable sort of mechanical device, from the smallest precision tool to guided missiles and aircraft.

The trading activities of the medieval town were organised into guilds.

* * *

FACING PAGE: *The Charred Cross and the Cross of Nails in the sanctuary of the Ruins focus the purpose of the Ministry of Coventry Cathedral—Resurrection through Sacrifice.*

RIGHT: *The exterior of the lovely Chapel of Unity. It is dedicated to the unity of Christian churches and was planned to create an impression of a crusader's tent.*

These were as ancient and as honourable as the City of London guilds. Many had their own chapels in St. Michael's, namely the Smiths, the Dyers, the Cappers, the Grocers. Of these, only the Cappers retains its meeting place in the cathedral—in the Cappers' Room. This is on the south side of the Ruins and was beautifully restored after the war.

It is of interest that this room served as the British Broadcasting Corporation's broadcasting studio in the cathedral for a year before the present permanent studio in the undercroft of the new cathedral was occupied. Coventry was the first cathedral to have a broadcasting studio within it.

The history of the diocese of Coventry dates from 1100 when it provided, in the great monastic church of St. Mary, one of the episcopal seats of the vast diocese of Coventry and Lichfield which extended from the Ribble to the Thames. St. Mary's Cathedral, being within the Benedictine monastery, together with the churches of the Greyfriars and Whitefriars, was destroyed soon after the suppression of the monasteries and guilds by Henry VIII in 1538. The centre of the diocese moved then to Lichfield, whose bishop held jurisdiction over Coventry until 1836, when the diocese of Worcester incorporated the area of the later diocese of Coventry. It was in 1918 that Coventry once again became the centre of its own diocese. The city's genius for invention made it a natural centre for the motor and aircraft industries, and the demands of the first world war upon its industries caused its population to develop rapidly. It was in acknowledgment of the growth of its population, with the consequent demands upon its church life, that in 1918 the diocese was recreated, and the ancient parish church of St. Michael was made the cathedral.

Enough remains of this famous church to appreciate the beauty of its proportions. From the 14th century to the end of the 15th the great church of St. Michael benefited both by the wealth of Coventry benefactors, and by the richness of contemporary architecture. The noble west tower was built between 1373 and 1394, when the choir and apse were also built. The erection of the nave and inner aisles occupied the next half-century, during which the spire was added to the tower. The spire was completed in 1433.

The beautiful cathedral church was reduced to ruins in one air raid during the night of Thursday, 14th November, 1940, when Coventry suffered the longest air-raid of any one night on any British city during the second world war. The cathedral was destroyed by fire bombs and not by high-explosives. In consequence, the outer walls and the tower and spire remained intact, but the wooden roof, the heavy oak ceiling, the pews, the floor and the screen were completely destroyed. Two precious relics grew out of, rather than survived, the destruction. A few days after the bombing, two irregular pieces of the oak roof beams—charred but still solid for lengths of 12 feet and 8 feet respectively—were tied together by wire, fixed in an old dustbin filled with

* * *

LEFT: *The Queen's Steps lead from the Ruins to the Porch. Through the Porch runs St. Michael's Avenue along which pass the citizens of Coventry going about their daily tasks.*

FACING PAGE: *The 'west' screen is a vast wall of clear glass panels incised with an array of figures of angels and saints designed and engraved by John Hutton.*

anti-incendiary bomb sand, and set up at the east end of the Ruins. This "Charred Cross" is now world-famous, and was placed behind the stone altar in the sanctuary of the Ruins, having as its reredos the carving of the simple words FATHER FORGIVE. In 1978 because of the fear of vandalism it was moved into the undercroft and a replica put in its place. The second relic of the ancient church which became a spark of life in the ministry of the new church is the "Cross of Nails". As the roof burnt, large 14th-century hand-forged nails which had fastened together its beams littered the ruined floor of the sanctuary. The following morning the inspiration came to form three of the nails into the shape of a Cross. This Cross has become the symbol of Coventry Cathedral's Ministry of International Reconciliation. Crosses of Nails have been formally presented to many centres throughout the world where there has been a response to the efforts of the cathedral to establish links of fellowship to study the meaning of Christian Reconciliation in a divided world, and to encourage exchanges of young people to engage in that study. Among the centres where Crosses exist are Oslo, Ottobeuren, Hamburg, Kiel, Munster, Berlin, Dresden, Volgograd (previously known as Stalingrad), as well as several in Africa, Asia, America, Canada and Australia.

The decision to rebuild the cathedral was made on the day following the destruction of the old church, though it was to be sixteen years before its foundation stone was eventually laid. Meanwhile the life of the cathedral continued. The rubble in the ruins was cleared, the sanctuary prepared as described on this page and two underground chapels were repaired and furnished—one as "the Cathedral", the other as a Chapel of Unity for all Christians, though, being the larger of the two, it served also for the major Sunday services of the cathedral congregation. It was in the tiny east crypt chapel, known as the Wyley Chapel in memory of a distinguished Coventry family, that canons were installed and where the bishop's throne was placed. It could therefore be claimed that until the undercroft of the new cathedral came into use in 1958, this was the smallest cathedral in the world. The chapel, with its entry now from St. Michael's Avenue, and not from the Ruins, is regularly in use. The west crypt chapel was used as a choir practice room 1962–63 but is now again in use as the Chapel of the Cross. In it are to be found the illuminated cross designed by Geoffrey Clarke (and used 1959–62 in the temporary chapel under the new building), the Stalingrad Ikon and the Ebony Crucifix. The chapel has a beautiful vaulted roof, and if not open can be seen on request.

From the time that it was cleared for use as an "open-air cathedral" the nave of the Ruins was regularly filled with large congregations for special services. The tradition has now been established of having a service of Holy Communion at the High Altar of the Ruins "early in the morning while it was yet dark"—at 6 a.m. on Easter Day, and at 7 a.m. on Whit-Sunday.

* * *

LEFT: *The interior of the Chapel of Unity. The slender windows were designed by Margaret Traherne and were the gift of the German Evangelical churches. The marble mosaic floor, given by the people of Sweden, was designed by Einar Forseth.*

RIGHT: *Holy Communion in Coventry Cathedral. The beautiful vestments worn by the clergy were specially designed by John Piper.*

BLOOD
ETERNAL LIFE

From the beginning of the new vision of a resurgent cathedral, gifts arrived from far and near, from those who wished to share in its fellowship. From Tanganyika, a black ebony crucifix carved by 18-year-old Fundi Kasanga; from Blundell's School (where Bishop Neville Gorton of Coventry had been headmaster) the statue of Christ—the work of a 17-year-old schoolboy, Alain John, who was later killed in 1943 while serving in the Royal Air Force. From Kweilin in China a carved piece of the font of a church destroyed by Japanese bombers. From Kiel an ancient stone from St. Nicholas Church, and later the money to inaugurate the cathedral library. From Jerusalem (Jordan) a carved stone of fellowship, and later the great boulder from Bethlehem which is the cathedral font. From Stalingrad a beautiful ikon. From the late Dowager Marchioness of Reading, the processional Cross as a memorial to the Women's Voluntary Service. From the late Queen Mary an exquisite bible she had received on the occasion of her wedding. From Hong Kong a gift of Communion vestments. From Sweden the marble mosaic floor of the Chapel of Unity, and also the five stained glass windows at the "north" entrance to the Lady Chapel. From Denmark the narwhal tusk for the bishop's crozier. From Canada £10,000 towards the cost of the organ. From Germany two generous gifts, one specially to pay for the windows of the Chapel of Unity. From many benefactors in Coventry came large sums of money to provide some of the great artistic features of the cathedral and also to endow its music and its ministry.

These are gifts selected largely at random and the list does not pretend

* * *

FACING PAGE: *Four of the ten majestic nave windows which depict the Destiny of Man and the Revelation of God. They are angled so that their full beauty can best be seen from the High Altar. Particular windows were given by the Berlin Philharmonic Orchestra, the Warwickshire Freemasons and the Schoolchildren of Warwickshire.*

RIGHT: *The Bishop's Throne. Above it is the bishop's mitre designed by Elizabeth Frink and beautifully wrought in gilded copper. It is decorated with nuts and bolts symbolising the industrial interests of the Coventry diocese.*

to be comprehensive. Let these, however, speak for the world interest in this cathedral which has become for millions a symbol of the hope of Reconciliation in the name of Jesus Christ in our divided world and society.

This central idea of Reconciliation was born in the sanctuary of the Ruins, where the Charred Cross, the Cross of Nails and the words FATHER FORGIVE focused the purpose of the ministry of the cathedral. To expand and explain the meaning of these words in the context of this cathedral, and to release them from the restricted, though valid meaning of the divisions of the war, the "Litany of Reconciliation" has been placed in the sanctuary. Reproduced in many languages, it has become the central prayer of the world-wide International Fellowship of those who pray for peace. From this birthplace of this special ministry of Reconciliation grew the main ideas, both for the architecture and the ministry of the new Coventry Cathedral.

Entering the new cathedral, one is immediately challenged by the significance of the gigantic and majestic figure of Christ, declaring that the cathedral stands before all else for reconciliation between Christ—and Me. The worship, and the pattern of the services, and the experiments in the use of every possible means of reaching the popular mind, are all designed to effect this aspect of Reconciliation which is primary to all others—that between every man and woman on the one hand, and God on the other.

But because in 1940 Christians in Coventry were challenged dramatically to say and do something about the situation of division and hatred which accompanied the destruction of the city and the cathedral, the other principal contexts of division in our modern society could not be ignored in a cathedral which set out to be a centre of Reconciliation.

The first and obvious context was international. As an experiment, a small International Centre was established in the converted coal cellar and organ-blowing chamber under the sanctuary. It was opened in January, 1960, by Dr. Otto Dibelius, Bishop of Berlin, and furnished by an anonymous donor in Berlin who had lost his entire family in an air-raid on Berlin. So full of promise were the first two years of the Centre's life that it was beautifully extended in the autumn and winter of 1961–62 by a very remarkable team of young Christians from Germany. Under the title "Aktion Sühnezeichen" (Action Reconciliation), they gave up their paid employment for six months, and using money contributed by individual Christians from all over Germany, restored the old vestries as an extension of the International Centre. The

★ ★ ★

LEFT: *Two of the five Swedish windows at the 'north' entrance to the Lady Chapel. They were designed by Einar Forseth and given by Sweden. That on the left embodies the Royal coat of arms and the national emblems; the other symbolises Christian fellowship between the Churches of Sweden and the Anglican Church.*

FACING PAGE: *The Lady Chapel at the 'east' end of the cathedral. The lower part of the tapestry acts as a reredos to the altar. The striking screen was added in 1965 to enclose the chapel area.*

Centre now comprises a reception room, a lounge, a canteen, a library and an oratory, with an information centre. By doing this, the sixteen young Germans effected one of the most significant enterprises of Reconciliation ever conducted in Britain.

In 1965 the John F. Kennedy house was opened by Herr Willi Brandt, the Mayor of West Berlin. This provides accommodation for resident groups of young people from all over England and the world.

The second particular context of Reconciliation to which Coventry Cathedral has dedicated itself is in a divided Church. The Chapel of Unity stands as a witness to the Faith that we should, and the Hope that we shall, ALL BE ONE.

In 1944 the Coventry Cathedral Scheme for Christian Unity was launched. Out of the suffering of the war the idea was born that a place in the new cathedral could provide the centre—a chapel which was the common possession of all who wished to share in the enterprise—around which Christians of different denominations could grow together by mutual understanding, common prayer, and joint service in the community. A Christian Service Centre was planned as the first object and a Chapel of Unity for the second. In the event it was the Chapel of Unity which was built first. The Declaration of the Joint Council to administer the Chapel and the Centre was signed on the fifth anniversary of the destruction of the cathedral—14th November, 1945. It read:

"We, who, belonging to different Christian Communions, now set apart this place as a Chapel of Unity for the worship of God, acknowledge our Lord Jesus Christ as God and Saviour of the whole world. We have already experienced the grace of God through many years of work and prayer together: we believe that He has guided us to establish for His people a Christian Service Centre. We also believe that our undertaking will be in vain unless we seek His guidance, and it is for this purpose that we hallow this Chapel of Unity. We are true, each of us, to the traditions we have inherited, but we have learned to see more clearly the fullness of the one Christ as we have seen Him mirrored in others. Recognizing that there is but one Christ for all peoples and all times, we seek in the fellowship of this Chapel to take our part with the blessed company of all faithful people."

This Declaration was signed by twenty-one members of the Joint Council and witnessed by twelve representative Christian leaders from many different nations. It was reaffirmed in September, 1960, by the successors of those original members when the threshold stone THAT THEY ALL MAY BE ONE was laid at the entrance to the present chapel. The mosaic floor is the design of the famous Swedish artist, Einar Forseth, and the gift of Sweden, including among the contributors Their Majesties the King and Queen of Sweden. The ten windows in this chapel are the gift of the German Evangelical Churches.

The ministry of Reconciliation in an industrial area such as Coventry could not but include a centre of meeting between, and of prayer for, all who meet as employers and employees in the hundreds of factories in Coventry, great and small. This work is based on a Chapel of Industry, dedicated to Christ the Servant, standing at the north-east corner of the new cathedral, above the chapter house.

The Ruins and the new cathedral are designed to be, and are in fact, one unit and not two. The link between them is St. Michael's Porch, entered from the east by St. Michael's Steps,

Continued on page 14

FACING PAGE: *The mighty tapestry, the largest in the world, was designed by Graham Sutherland, O.M., and given by the late Alfred Harris, a resident of Coventry. It was woven in France and took 360,000 hours to make. The tapestry replaces the traditional east window and depicts Christ in Glory with 'Man' between his feet, and below, in sombre tones of grey and black, Christ crucified.*

ABOVE: *The High Altar is made of hammered concrete. The contrast of its stark simplicity against the bold colours of the tapestry emphasises its tremendous importance.*

over which is set the dominating statue of St. Michael defeating the Devil—the work of Sir Jacob Epstein. From the Ruins, the Queen's Steps lead to the porch, and it was by way of these steps that Her Majesty Queen Elizabeth II entered the cathedral for the Consecration Service in May, 1962. The porch is open to the public as a pedestrian way, and its central position in Coventry brings thousands daily beneath its roof.

In acknowledgment of the coming and going of so many, and of our determination that all that happens inside the cathedral shall be relevant to the world outside, the "west" wall is of clear glass. This great wall, incised by the late John Hutton, represents a great array of Angels and Patriarchs, Prophets, Apostles and Martyrs and others through whose faith we have inherited our faith and hope today. There are forty-two identifiable figures with three horizontal rows of flying angels.

Dominating the whole cathedral is the figure of Christ enthroned in Glory in the tapestry at the "east" end. This tapestry, designed by Graham Sutherland, and made by Pinton Frères at Felletin near Aubusson in France, measures about 74 feet in height, 38 feet in width and weighs slightly less than one ton.

To our right on entering the cathedral is the glorious symphony of colour of John Piper's design for the Baptistry window. "A blaze of light, framed and islanded in colour—the blaze of light symbolizing the Holy Spirit, which is the motif of the whole design."

Beneath the window, starkly in contrast to the radiant beauty of its background, is the font—a rough three-ton boulder from Bethlehem. It was brought by great goodwill—at every stage of its progress until its arrival on Christmas Eve, 1960, in Coventry, freely and without charge to the cathedral—from a hillside outside Bethlehem, beside the road in the valley of Barakat, the Valley of Blessedness. Thus, the most modern cathedral has the most ancient font, and a physical link with "the Rock from whence we are hewn".

Opposite the font is the entrance to the Chapel of Unity, appearing like a stage—which in fact is what it is. Here plays are presented which articulate contemporary problems which the Christian faith can show the way to solving. The use of this part of the cathedral as a theatre gives more freedom for the presentation of plays than would be possible if they were presented only in the chancel.

Facing us now as we look towards the High Altar and the tapestry beyond it are the eight great texts accompanied by the primitive Christian symbols. Carved by Ralph Beyer in irregular letters, the suggestion is conveyed that in this modern cathedral we nonetheless acknowledge our dependence on the original truths of our Faith. For these are the great texts

* * *

LEFT: *The theme of Coventry Cathedral of Resurrection through Sacrifice is repeated on the High Altar with the glorious silver-gilt Cross symbolizing Sacrifice.*

which conveyed the Christian Faith among the early converts to the Faith; these are the symbols carved on the walls of the caves under Rome, and both still speak of the same Faith as is declared in this cathedral consecrated nearly 2,000 years later.

The ten windows of the nave are hidden from direct view on entry, but an impression of their brilliance will have reached us by the kaleidoscope of reflected colour on the facing white walls, and by the reflections of the windows in the black marble floor of the aisles. These nave windows are 70 feet high and progress in pairs from font to altar. The first pair, Green, describes Beginnings. The second, Red, describes God's Intervention in His Creation. The third, Multi-coloured, speaks of Conflict and Struggle. The fourth pair, deep Blue and Purple, describes Maturity. The final pair, shedding their Golden colours on the altar, speaks of Ultimate Reality. They are the work of a team of three men from the Royal College of Art—Geoffrey Clark, Keith New, and their leader, Lawrence Lee.

The High Altar is hammered concrete—simple, stark, strong. It is the most important piece of furniture in the cathedral. In most churches this is conveyed by the beautification of the altar and the use of frontals. In this cathedral such treatment would lose the altar in the colours of the tapestry behind it. Hence it is emphasised not by beautification but by simplification.

Behind the High Altar is the Lady Chapel. In 1965 a screen, designed by Sir Basil Spence and given by the Friends of Coventry Cathedral, was added in order to divide the chapel area from the visitors' route that runs through it. To the right of the Lady Chapel is the Chapel of Christ in Gethsemane, enclosed by a beautiful wrought-iron screen in the shape of a Crown of Thorns. This is the gift of the Royal Engineers, in whose workshops at Chatham it was made.

At this point the Chapel of Christ The Servant adjoins the cathedral. This was originally intended as a guild chapel, but because of the great importance of industry in Coventry it was made a centre for the chaplains working among the industrial community in the City and Diocese and thus it is also known as the Chapel of Industry. Designed by the architect, it is circular in shape and the windows are of clear glass so that those within the chapel will be ever mindful of the industrial scene outside. The beautiful oak altar table which is inlaid with box wood, and the stone base, were made and given by the apprentices of Coventry Technical College, and it was they who carved the gilded inscription, I AM AMONG YOU AS ONE THAT SERVES. Above the table is a Cross rising from a Crown of Thorns made by Geoffrey Clark.

The undercroft contains many features designed to bring together those who would value the cathedral as a centre of meeting, including a reception

Continued on page 18

* * *

RIGHT: *The High Altar Candlesticks. Made of pottery they stand taller than a man—three on each side of the High Altar. They are believed to be the largest 'thrown' pots in existence and were designed by Hans Coper.*

ABOVE: *The interior of the Chapel of Christ the Servant with its Cross and Crown of Thorns made by Geoffrey Clark above the oak altar table given by the apprentices of Coventry Technical College.* FACING PAGE: *The Chapel of Christ in Gethsemane. At the entrance is the extremely beautiful wrought-iron grill symbolizing the Crown of Thorns. Beyond is the reredos and to the right a blue mosaic panel depicting the three disciples asleep.*

room for distinguished guests, called the "Navy Room" to acknowledge this gift from the Royal Navy which furnished it, and a well-equipped lecture room. It also contains a sound broadcasting studio and a television control room from which the intricate network of wiring for cameras and the extremely adequate television lighting equipment permanently installed in the nave is controlled. This was generously given by the British Broadcasting Corporation.

In addition there is an assembly hall which can be used for gatherings for light refreshments and talk after events in the cathedral, and a restaurant for the daily provision of meals and breakfast after early Communion, and for use as a social centre for Coventry Christians. These are some of the features through which it is hoped the new cathedral will become a focal point for the unity of the whole community, and vindicate the faith contained in the inscription across the floor of the nave at the entrance:

TO THE GLORY OF GOD
THIS CATHEDRAL BURNT
NOVEMBER 14 AD 1940
IS NOW REBUILT 1962

Coventry Cathedral was consecrated on Friday, 25th May, 1962. The congregation of 2,300 within the cathedral was headed by Her Majesty Queen Elizabeth II, accompanied by Her Royal Highness the Princess Margaret and the Earl of Snowdon. A further 2,000 people were seated in stands in the Ruins. The Right Reverend Cuthbert Bardsley, Lord Bishop of Coventry, performed the acts of consecration and His Grace the Archbishop of Canterbury preached the sermon. The consecration was concluded the following morning by the first celebration of Holy Communion during which a record of the craftsmen who had built the cathedral was laid on the altar.

During the three weeks of Festival which followed the consecration, many special services were held. These were arranged to embrace the interests of local government, international affairs, industry and agriculture, education and medicine, the old and the young, the armed forces and the arts.

* * *

The greatest single objective of the Ministry of Coventry Cathedral is to establish a creative relationship with the community in which it is set. There are many community structures which the parish system cannot begin remotely to influence. Among these are industry, the arts, commerce, social service, local goverment, science, technology and so on. The Ministry of Coventry Cathedral is so organised as to experiment on the widest possible front to find "points of entry" into these definable community structures and to learn the fundamental principles about human relations of the future which they raise.

To this end the staff of Coventry Cathedral consists of a team of men and women working in the following main departments, but held together by a

Continued on page 22

* * *

LEFT: *The lectern is made from satin-finish bronze and Afrormosia wood. The fine cast-bronze eagle surmounting it is by Elizabeth Frink.*

RIGHT: *Two of the eight Tablets of the Word which are a striking feature in the Nave. The beautiful uneven letters emphasise the primitive origins of the texts which contain the Truth about Christ's revelation of God.*

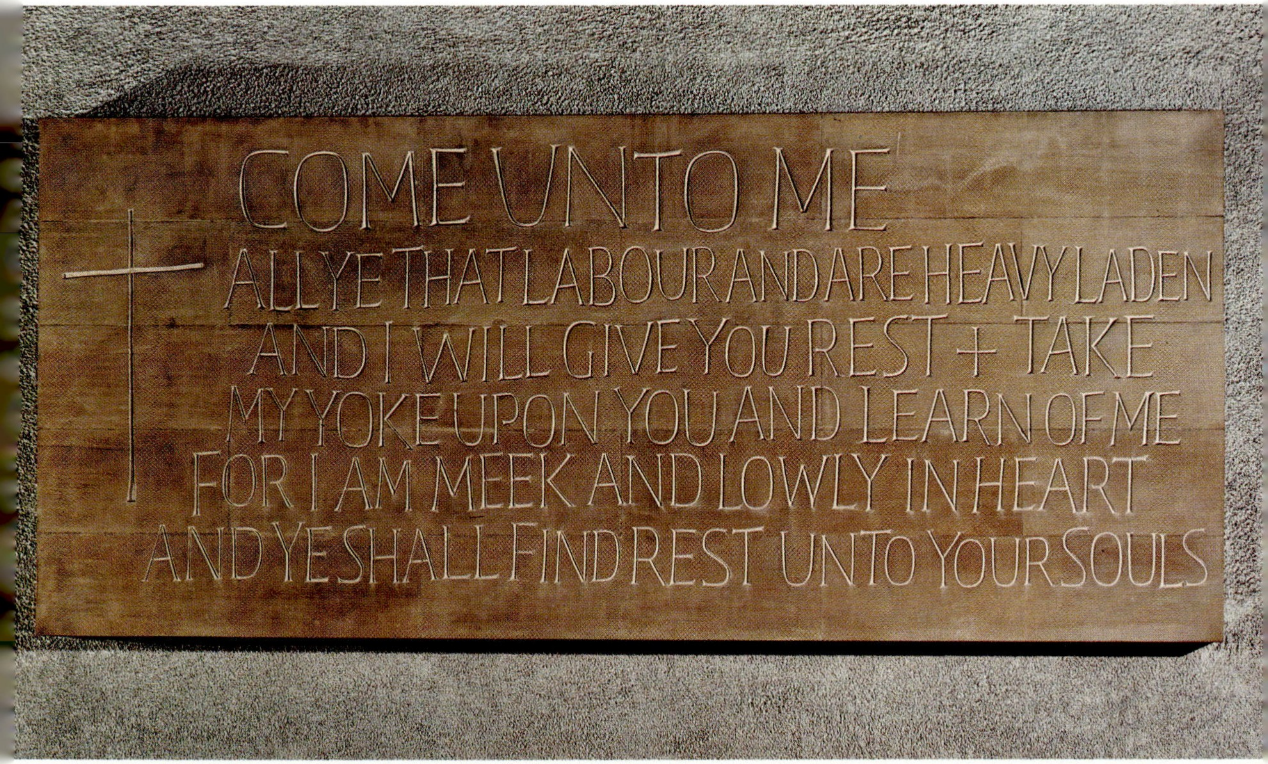

COME UNTO ME
ALL YE THAT LABOUR AND ARE HEAVY LADEN
AND I WILL GIVE YOU REST + TAKE
MY YOKE UPON YOU AND LEARN OF ME
FOR I AM MEEK AND LOWLY IN HEART
AND YE SHALL FIND REST UNTO YOUR SOULS

THE SON OF MAN IS COME
TO SEEK AND TO SAVE
THAT WHICH WAS LOST
THE GOOD SHEPHERD
GIVETH HIS LIFE FOR THE SHEEP +

ABOVE: *The Font, mounted on a bronze stem, is a huge boulder roughly hewn from a hillside in the Valley of Blessedness, near Bethlehem.*

RIGHT: *One of the great glories of Coventry Cathedral is the Baptistry Window. This immense curved structure of stained glass and stone floods the nave with a breathtaking blaze of colour. The theme is the light of the Holy Spirit. It was designed by John Piper and made by Patrick Reyntiens.*

closely integrated relationship among themselves; industry; commerce; social services; education; sociology; music and culture generally; international youth, national youth and local youth; liturgy; Christian unity; international affairs and the general administration of the cathedral. This experiment is conducted in the belief that it is from some form of team structure that the Ministry of the future will emerge.

In 1947 the Reconstruction Committee was entrusted by the Cathedral Council with the task of rebuilding the cathedral, and a design competition open to architects of the British Commonwealth was held. There were 219 entries. In August 1951 the design submitted by Mr. (now Sir) Basil Spence won the competition. In their report the three assessors, themselves distinguished architects, declared: "... we not only feel that it is the best design submitted, but that it is the one which shows that the author has qualities of spirit and imagination of the highest order".

The cathedral authorities accepted and endorsed this decision. John Laing Construction Ltd. were appointed general contractors, with Ove Arup and Partners as the structural engineers. Some eighty other firms and organisations supplied materials, services and furnishings. The work of reconstruction began on 8th June 1954. The laying of the foundations started on 7th March 1955 and the cathedral was virtually completed on 28th April 1962 when the "flying Cross" was lowered on to the flèche from a Royal Air Force helicopter.

At peak periods some five hundred skilled and unskilled workers in many crafts and trades were variously engaged in building and equipping the cathedral. The spirit of goodwill, indeed devotion, which prevailed among these workers was such that never during the eight years was there any labour unrest. The cathedral cost about one million three hundred and fifty thousand pounds. Of this sum one million pounds was war damage compensation.

John F. Kennedy House, designed by Sir Basil Spence, was completed in 1965. The expanding Ministry calls for more ancillary buildings.

* * *

ABOVE: *The 'south' side of the cathedral. On the left are the Ruins with the Porch linking the 14th-century and 20th-century buildings. Beyond is the sculpture of St. Michael and the Devil, the Baptistry window, the nave windows and the Chapel of Christ the Servant.*

RIGHT: *This magnificent bronze sculpture by Sir Jacob Epstein depicts St. Michael, patron saint of the cathedral, defeating the Devil. In 1969 one of Epstein's earliest works 'Ecce Homo' was given to the cathedral by his trustees. It now stands in the Ruins.*

ABOVE: *The Chapel of Christ the Servant is also called the Chapel of Industry. The chapel is joined to the cathedral by a wide corridor, and beneath it at ground level is the Chapter House.*

LEFT: *John F. Kennedy House stands in the grounds of the cathedral. Here the young people from all over the world who come to take part in youth courses and conferences live and work while staying in Coventry. Opposite Kennedy House in Hilltop is Bardsley House—the Cathedral Youth Community Centre. It is named after the Rt. Rev. Cuthbert Bardsley, Bishop of Coventry from 1956 to 1976.*

* * *

ACKNOWLEDGMENTS

All the photographs in this book except that on p. i cover, which is by P. W. & L. Thompson of Coventry, and that on p. 7, which is by Richard Sadler, AIIP, FRSA, are by Gerald Newbery, FIIP, FRPS.

SBN 85372 101 7